CELEBRATING THE CITY OF SHANGHAI

Celebrating the City of Shanghai

Walter the Educator

Silent King Books

SILENT KING BOOKS

SKB

Copyright © 2024 by Walter the Educator

All rights reserved. No part of this book may be reproduced in any manner whatsoever without written permission except in the case of brief quotations embodied in critical articles and reviews.

First Printing, 2024

Disclaimer
This book is a literary work; the story is not about specific persons, locations, situations, and/or circumstances unless mentioned in a historical context. Any resemblance to real persons, locations, situations, and/or circumstances is coincidental. This book is for entertainment and informational purposes only. The author and publisher offer this information without warranties expressed or implied. No matter the grounds, neither the author nor the publisher will be accountable for any losses, injuries, or other damages caused by the reader's use of this book. The use of this book acknowledges an understanding and acceptance of this disclaimer.

Celebrating the City of Shanghai is a little collectible souvenir book that belongs to the Celebrating Cities Book Series by Walter the Educator. Collect them all and more books at WaltertheEducator.com

USE THE EXTRA SPACE TO TAKE NOTES AND DOCUMENT YOUR MEMORIES

SHANGHAI

In the embrace of the Yangtze, where whispers kiss the sea,

Celebrating the City of Shanghai

A symphony of skyscrapers, Shanghai stands with majesty.

She, a phoenix risen from ancient embers,

Her spirit a dance of yesteryears' members.

Cobblestone streets where old tales reside,

In alleyways where histories confide,

Temples whispering secrets of dynasties gone,

In Shanghai, a city where futures are drawn.

Her rivers, serpentine, carry dreams anew,

Past bridges that wear the morning dew.

Bund's colonial grace, a relic of the past,

Celebrating the City of Shanghai

Neon lights of Pudong, a future forecast.

The silk that flows through time's gentle hand,

Unfolds in Shanghai, a tapestry grand.

Lanterns glow in ancient streets,

Whispers of history the air repeats,

Old tea houses in hidden lanes,

Guard secrets of dynastic reigns.

Markets alive with colors so bright,

Red lanterns sway, guiding the night.

From the lullabies of the ancient walled town,

To the electric hum where modern towers crown,

Shanghai's heart pulses in relentless beat,

A mosaic of lives on every street.

Celebrating the City of Shanghai

She's a canvas where cultures blend,

A place where East and West transcend.

In the alleys, you hear the merchant's call,

In the towers, ambitions that never stall.

The scent of jasmine mingles with the sea's salt,

In tea houses where elders their stories exalt.

In the shadow of temples where incense swirls,

Children play in the dance of new world pearls.

Trams clang through the veins of this jewel,

Waking the city from morning's cool.

Street vendors' cries, a melody unique,

In the labyrinth of streets, secrets peek.

to Shanghai, a city grand,

A place where dreams and reality stand.

A celebration of spirit, in every strand,

Shanghai, forever, a timeless land.

Celebrating the City of Shanghai

Walter the Educator is one of the pseudonyms for Walter Anderson. Formally educated in Chemistry, Business, and Education, he is an educator, an author, a diverse entrepreneur, and he is the son of a disabled war veteran. "Walter the Educator" shares his time between educating and creating. He holds interests and owns several creative projects that entertain, enlighten, enhance, and educate, hoping to inspire and motivate you.

Follow, find new works, and stay up to date with Walter the Educator™
at WaltertheEducator.com

www.ingramcontent.com/pod-product-compliance
Lightning Source LLC
LaVergne TN
LVHW012050070526
838201LV00082B/3903